Jumpstarters for Nutrition and Exercise

Short Daily Warm-ups for the Classroom

By
Pat St. Onge and Dr. Joseph Kunicki

COPYRIGHT © 2009 Mark Twain Media, Inc.

ISBN 978-1-58037-487-3

Printing No. CD-404106

Visit us at www.carsondellosa.com

Mark Twain Media, Inc., Publishers
Distributed by Carson-Dellosa Publishing Company, Inc.

Table of Contents

Introduction to the Teacher

Jumpstarters for Nutrition and Exercise provides daily reviews for skills previously learned by students as they prepare for the day's lessons. Each page contains five warm-ups, one for each day of the school week. Students will use problem-solving skills as they compare and contrast, analyze issues, and gain additional insights into making better food and exercise choices.

Suggestions for using warm-up activities:

- Copy and cut apart one page each week. Give students one warm-up activity each day at the beginning of class.

- Give each student a copy of the entire page to keep in their binders to complete as assigned.

- Make transparencies of individual warms-ups and complete activities as a group.

- Put copies of warm-ups in a learning center for students to complete on their own when they have a few extra minutes.

- Use warm-ups as homework assignments.

- Use warm-ups as questions in a review game.

- Keep some warm-ups on hand to use when the class has a few extra minutes before dismissal.

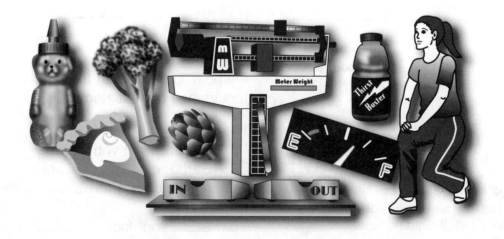

Nutrition and Exercise Warm-ups: Diet

Name/Date _____

Diet 1

What does the word "diet" mean? Circle the correct number.

a. Diet refers to everything you eat and drink.
b. Diet refers to cutting back on food intake to lose weight.
c. Diet refers to food restrictions because of health.

1. a only   2. a & b   3. a & c   4. b & c   5. a, b, & c

Name/Date _____

Diet 2

Write "T" for true or "F" for false.

1. _____ What you eat is not particularly important if you get enough exercise.
2. _____ The typical American diet provides all the nutrients you need.
3. _____ It's okay to eat junk food if you are young and healthy.
4. _____ Diets are for overweight people and health nuts.
5. _____ Eating healthy costs too much money.

Name/Date _____

Diet 3

Did you know? Obesity is the #1 health problem in the United States.

Even though Americans have some of the healthiest food in the world available to them, why do you think obesity is increasing at an alarming rate? Answer on your own paper.

Name/Date _____

Diet 4

You've heard this before—is it good advice?
1. Eat all your vegetables. (YES / NO)
2. Clean your plate; children are starving in China. (YES / NO)
3. Try a bite; how do you know if you like it or not? (YES / NO)
4. Eat what's on your plate or you won't get any dessert. (YES / NO)
5. Don't eat so fast—slow down and chew. (YES / NO)

Name/Date _____

Diet 5

Slogans are an easy way to remember ideas. Match the letters to their correct slogans.

a. lips, hips
b. in, garbage
c. Eat to live
d. Drink, chew
e. eat

1. _____, don't live to eat.
2. You are what you _____.
3. Garbage _____, _____ out.
4. A moment on the _____, a lifetime on the _____!
5. _____ your food and _____ your drink.

Nutrition and Exercise Warm-ups: Feed Your Brain

Name/Date _____

Feed Your Brain 1

Fill in the blanks.

> peak   essential
> regulate nutrition

Your brain depends on you to provide the _____ it needs in order to _____ the complex body systems that keep your body operating at _____ performance. Healthy eating and regular exercise are _____ to having a healthy brain.

Name/Date _____

Feed Your Brain 2

Draw a line to match each term to the best definition.

1. neurotransmitters
2. essential vitamins
3. enzymes and hormones
4. serotonin
5. amino acids

a. building blocks of protein
b. used by the brain to regulate mood
c. message delivery system
d. only gotten from foods
e. proteins

Name/Date _____

Feed Your Brain 3

Match these "brain foods" with the best descriptions.

1. _____ These "brain foods" are an excellent source of Omega 3 fatty acids.
2. _____ These "brain foods" are a great source of antioxidants.
3. _____ These "brain foods" provide antioxidants that satisfy a craving for sweets.
4. _____ This "brain food" helps keep your brain running smoothly.

a. blueberries, strawberries, cherries, and kiwis
b. cod, salmon, shrimp
c. fresh water
d. spinach, broccoli, and Brussels sprouts

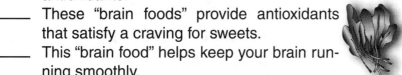

Name/Date _____

Feed Your Brain 4

Mark "T" for true or "F" for false.

1. _____ Your emotions can affect what you eat.
2. _____ Your emotions can affect how much you eat.
3. _____ What you eat can affect your emotions.
4. _____ Food and emotions do not influence each other.

Name/Date _____

Feed Your Brain 5

Write "H" if these common reactions to stress are healthy or "N" if they are not.

1. _____ Overeat by using food as comfort.
2. _____ Eat far less or not at all.
3. _____ Stay too busy to notice the stress.
4. _____ Take time to care for yourself.
5. _____ Sleep more or very little.
6. _____ Go for a walk.
7. _____ Use alcohol to relieve stress.

Nutrition and Exercise Warm-ups: Exercise

Name/Date _____

Exercise 1

Name the part of the body that each of these conditions affects, and how exercise may improve the condition.

1. Osteoporosis: _____
2. Arthritis: _____
3. Blood Pressure: _____
4. Depression: _____
5. Muscle weakness: _____

Name/Date _____

Exercise 2

Can you unscramble these aerobic exercises?

1. pmunjgi proe _____
2. lwkigan _____
3. gigojgn _____
4. lyccgin _____
5. srosc ytonucr inisgk

_____

Name/Date _____

Exercise 3

How much physical activity is recommended for people ages 6–18? Circle the correct choice.

a. at least 30 minutes a day
b. at least 60 minutes a day
c. several hours a day.
c. at least 30 minutes 5 days a week.

Name/Date _____

Exercise 4

A pound of fat represents approximately how many stored calories? Circle the correct choice.

a. 1,500 calories
b. 300 calories
c. 3,500 calories
d. 700 calories

Name/Date _____

Exercise 5

Walking at a brisk rate (about 1 mile in 15 minutes) burns about 100 calories. How long would you need to walk to work off a pound of fat? How many miles would you have to walk? Answer on your own paper.

Nutrition and Exercise Warm-ups: Proper Rest

Name/Date _____

Proper Rest 1

People often say to wait an hour between eating and going for a swim, but when should you stop eating meals before going to sleep to allow for good digestion?

a. several hours

b. 30 minutes

c. 1 hour

d. eat right up to bedtime

Name/Date _____

Proper Rest 2

Draw a line to match the amount of sleep recommended for these ages.

1. kids 3–5 years old
2. 5–12 years old
3. 12–18 years old
4. Adults over 18

a. 10–11 hours
b. 8–9 hours
c. 7–8 hours
d. 11–12 hours

Name/Date _____

Proper Rest 3

True or False: Sleep assists the following functions.

1. Growth hormones stimulate cell reproduction and repair when you rest. _____

2. Physical healing slows down during sleep. _____

3. Red blood cells remove wastes from your cells at night. _____

4. Sleeping creates the need to sleep more. _____

5. Your mind sorts and processes the events of the day while you sleep. _____

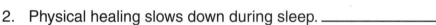

Name/Date _____

Proper Rest 4

If you are having trouble sleeping, which of the following drinks would help you fall asleep?

1. a cola
2. warm milk
3. coffee
4. chamomile tea

Do some research. What makes warm milk such an effective nighttime drink? Write your answer on your own paper.

Name/Date _____

Proper Rest 5

Given what you know about food and sleep, list three things you can do to help your body prepare for sleep at night.

a. _____

b. _____

c. _____

Nutrition and Exercise Warm-ups: The New Food Pyramid—Grains

*Refer to Food Pyramid chart on Appendix page 39.

Name/Date _____

Grains 1

Grains are a staple (basic) food for humans the world over. Whole grains provide a healthy source of carbohydrates, which release simple and complex sugars slowly to give us long-lasting energy.

On your own paper, list at least four grains commonly used in cereals and breads. Can you name more than four?

Name/Date _____

Grains 2

Match each part of the grain to its nutrients:

____ 1. endosperm   ____ 2. germ

____ 3. bran

a. high in fat, minerals, vitamin E, and B vitamins
b. the layer with fiber, B vitamins, protein, and minerals
c. the highest content of starchy carbs

Name/Date _____

Grains 3

Unscramble this two-word term for whole-grain foods.

y a m e r p b o x r h o t a c l e d s c

_____

Name/Date _____

Grains 4

Which snacks are the better choices of unrefined carbohydrates? Check the better choices.

1. popcorn ____   2. cupcakes ____
3. corn chips ____   4. potato chips ____
5. rice cakes ____   6. oatmeal cookie ____
7. doughnuts ____   8. bran muffins ____

Name/Date _____

Grains 5

Many cultures brought their favorite traditional ways to prepare grains with them when they immigrated to America, where these foods have become widely available to everyone. What popular grain dish do you associate with each of the following cuisines?

1. Italian _____   2. Mexican _____   3. Chinese _____
4. Indian _____   5. Greek _____   6. Jewish _____
7. African _____   8. Scotch-Irish _____   9. French _____
10. German _____

Ask your classmates to describe a dish from their family's ethnic tradition.

Nutrition and Exercise Warm-ups: The New Food Pyramid—Vegetables

*Refer to Food Pyramid chart on Appendix page 39.

Name/Date _____

Vegetables 1

On your own paper, draw a rainbow with six bands, one for each color below. Then fill in the bands with vegetables that match that color. When you are done, shade in the rainbow with the correct colors.

Red, Orange, Yellow, Green, Blue, Violet

Name/Date _____

Vegetables 2

Different parts of vegetable plants may be edible. On your own paper, list at least one vegetable that represents each edible part of a vegetable plant.

1. roots and tubers
2. stalks
3. leaves
4. flowers
5. fruit (what the plant produces)
6. seeds and seedpods

Name/Date _____

Vegetables 3

Unscramble these names of vegetables:

1. agatabur _____
2. lauragu _____
3. qushas _____
4. denevi _____
5. hitrkeaco _____
6. bkorhail _____
7. ciuzihnc _____
8. oiwlacufrel _____

Name/Date _____

Vegetables 4

Name three things that vegetables contribute to your diet.

1. _____
2. _____
3. _____

Name/Date _____

Vegetables 5

Vegetable are "nutrient-dense" foods. What does this mean?

_____
_____
_____
_____
_____

Nutrition and Exercise Warm-ups:
The New Food Pyramid—Fruits

*Refer to Food Pyramid chart on Appendix page 39.

Name/Date _____

_____

Fruits 1

Can you guess what I am? You may think I'm a vegetable, but I'm actually a fruit!

Hints:
- You'll get plenty of potassium, vitamin A, alpha carotene, beta carotene, and other nutrients plus a big dose of fiber when you eat me.

- Use me fresh or canned.

- Bake my seeds and eat those for a healthy snack.

- I can be added to pies, cakes, bread, or you can even make me into soup!

What am I?

_____

(It's a fruit from the gourd family because it grows from a flower.)

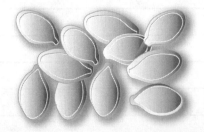

Name/Date _____

Fruits 2

Fill in the blank.

Fruits and fruit juices can be used as a substitute for _____ in many recipes.

Name/Date _____

Fruits 3

How many servings of fruit per day are recommended for school age children? Check the USDA Food Pyramid or another source.

_____

Name/Date _____

Fruits 4

Fill in the blank.

 The sugars contained in fruits are called _____. Most people can easily digest this type of sugar.

Name/Date _____

Fruits 5

Can you think of ways to serve fruit at every meal by combining it with other foods? On your own paper, list ways to add fruit to your diet besides eating it whole. Be creative!

1. Breakfast
2. Lunch
3. Dinner
4. Desserts

Nutrition and Exercise Warm-ups:
The New Food Pyramid—Fats

*Refer to Food Pyramid chart on Appendix page 39.

Name/Date _____

Fats 1

These are some of the reasons why our body stores fat:

- Fat aids nervous system and brain function.
- Fat helps the absorption of the fat-soluble vitamins A, D, E, and K.
- Fats assist with the production of hormones.

List three additional ways fat benefits our bodies. _____

_____

_____

_____

Name/Date _____

Fats 2

1. What are the two main groups under which fats are classified?

   _____

2. Why is a high intake of saturated fat (also called trans-fat or hydrogenated fat) unhealthy?

   _____

   _____

   _____

Name/Date _____

Fats 3

Can you name sources of **saturated fats**? List them below.

_____

_____

_____

_____

Name/Date _____

Fats 4

Can you name sources of **unsaturated fats**? List them below.

_____

_____

_____

_____

Name/Date _____

Fats 5

All the body cells (including brain cells) use essential fatty acids, or EFAs, to carry out functions like improving vision, learning skills, and regulating mood. They also help protect us from diseases like some cancers and heart disease. We get EFAs from our diet because our bodies do not make them.

On your own paper, list three rich sources of EFAs.

Nutrition and Exercise Warm-ups: The New Food Pyramid—Milk Products

*Refer to Food Pyramid chart on Appendix page 39.

Name/Date _____

Milk Products 1

Fill in the blanks in the following sentence.

Milk products help to prevent a bone condition called _____. It is a reduction in bone _____ that weakens the bones, making them more likely to _____ and break.

Name/Date _____

Milk Products 2

In addition to calcium, magnesium, phosphorus, potassium, and protein, milk is a valuable source of this vitamin. (Circle the answer.)

a. Vitamin K   b. Vitamin C

c. Vitamin D   d. Vitamin B

Name/Date _____

Milk Products 3

The milk, or dairy, food group includes what other foods in addition to milk?

_____

_____

_____

_____

Name/Date _____

Milk Products 4

How many servings per day of dairy foods should you include in a healthy diet? _____

List some ideas of how you could include the milk group in every meal.

_____

_____

_____

Name/Date _____

Milk Products 5

Cholesterol is found in the blood, and is commonly referred to as "good" or "bad" cholesterol. Milk products can be high in cholesterol, since they come from animals. Low fat and skim milk products have less cholesterol than whole milk.

1. What are the two types of cholesterol? _____

2. Which is the "bad" cholesterol, and why is it "bad"? _____

_____

_____

Nutrition and Exercise Warm-ups:
The New Food Pyramid—Meats, Beans, & Nuts

*Refer to Food Pyramid chart on Appendix page 39.

Name/Date _____

Meats, Beans, & Nuts 1

Foods in the meat group are considered a prime source of one of the body's most important building blocks. Which one is it?

a. Micronutrients   b. Calcium

c. Omega 3 fatty acids   d. Protein

Name/Date _____

Meats, Beans, & Nuts 2

Fill in the blank.

Guidelines suggest limiting the amount of processed meats like hot dogs, sausage, ham, and cold cuts included in your daily diet because they contain high levels of _____.

Name/Date _____

Meats, Beans, & Nuts 3

A healthy diet might include several servings of fish each week in order to boost your intake of this important nutrient. Circle the best answer.

a. Vitamin K   b. Omega 3 fatty acids

c. Cholesterol   d. B vitamins

Name/Date _____

Meats, Beans, & Nuts 4

How can vegetarians (people who don't eat any meat) supplement their diets in order to get enough protein? Come up with some ideas, and list them on your own paper. Try to think of non-meat or non-animal sources of protein.

Name/Date _____
_____

Meats, Beans, & Nuts 5

List at least three different food resources in each category.

1. lean meat: _____
_____
_____

2. poultry: _____
_____

3. fresh fish: _____
_____
_____

4. canned fish: _____
_____
_____

5. shellfish: _____
_____
_____

6. nuts: _____
_____
_____

7. beans and peas: _____
_____
_____

Nutrition and Exercise Warm-ups:
The New Food Pyramid—Exercise

*Refer to Food Pyramid chart on Appendix page 39.

Name/Date _____

Exercise 1

Wait a minute ... exercise? The new food pyramid includes exercise as a category to emphasize the importance of exercise in a healthy lifestyle.

Unscramble the words that describe what the lack of exercise can lead to.

1. tibyose   _____

2. lemcus kawsesne _____

3. wolre nebo isedtyn _____

4. terah operslmb   _____

Name/Date _____

Exercise 2

How does exercise help your brain?

_____

_____

_____

_____

Name/Date _____

Exercise 3

Why exercise? How does exercise help you lose weight?

_____

_____

_____

_____

Name/Date _____

Exercise 4

True or False:

_____ Working out and playing sports are the only forms of exercise that help you lose weight.

Explain: _____

_____

_____

Name/Date _____

Exercise 5

Think of five things you can do TODAY to increase your activity level.

1. _____

2. _____

3. _____

4. _____

5. _____

Nutrition and Exercise Warm-ups: Serving Sizes

Name/Date _____

Serving Sizes 1

An average serving of meat or fish is 3–4 oz. This is about the size of ...

  a. a submarine sandwich bun   b. a deck of playing cards

  c. a notebook   d. a chalkboard eraser

> An easy way to learn the average serving sizes is to associate them with things you are familiar with.

Name/Date _____

Serving Sizes 2

An average serving of cooked vegetables is 4 oz. This is about the size of ...

  a. a soup bowl   b. an egg cup

  c. a small cupcake   d. a coffee mug

Name/Date _____

Serving Sizes 3

A large bagel is about the circumference of ...
(compare: a small bagel is about the size of a hockey puck.)

  a. a CD   b. a baseball

  c. a soup can   d. a coffee cup

Name/Date _____

Serving Sizes 4

A potato of average serving size (4 oz.) is about the size of ...

  a. a tennis ball   b. a soda can

  c. a computer mouse   d. a TV remote control

Name/Date _____

Serving Sizes 5

An average serving of peanut butter (2 TBSP.) is about the size of ...

  a. an egg   b. a whole peanut

  c. a peach   d. a ping-pong ball

> You can help yourself learn about servings by reading labels. You may be surprised to see that a single container may actually supply two to three servings!

Nutrition and Exercise Warm-ups: Balanced Meals

Name/Date _____

Balanced Meals 1

A balanced meal is:

a. 1/2 vegetables and 1/2 protein.

b. 1/2 grains, with a little protein and dairy.

c. 1/2 vegetables, 1/4 grains, and 1/4 protein.

d. close to 2/3 vegetables, 1/3 meat, and small amounts of the other groups.

Name/Date _____

Balanced Meals 2

On your own paper, write out a meal plan for a day based on the colors of the rainbow.

Name/Date _____

Balanced Meals 3

 You look in the cupboard for a snack and find the following items: potato chips, cookies, applesauce, nuts, chocolate cupcakes, popcorn, olives, cereal, yogurt-covered raisins, mini doughnuts, candy bars, and canned tuna.

Can you assemble a balanced snack? Which foods would you include in your snack?

_____

_____

Name/Date _____

Balanced Meals 4

You are traveling and need to grab a meal at a fast food chain. What might you order for a nutritious meal? What do you want to avoid? Why?

_____

_____

_____

Name/Date _____

Balanced Meals 5

Should you eat the same balanced meal every day? Why or why not?

_____

_____

_____

_____

14

Nutrition and Exercise Warm-ups: Empty Calories or Nutrient-Dense Food?

Name/Date _____

Empty Calories? 1

Are you starting your day with empty calories? Look up the sugar content of the cereals you eat regularly. Compare them to the sugar content of candy bars.

Think of nutrient-dense foods that you might eat instead of sugary cereals.

_____

_____

Name/Date _____

Empty Calories? 2

Select a snack: Circle the nutrient-dense food from each pair.

1. a. potato chips   b. baked potato

2. c. grape juice   d. grapes

3. e. gummy fruit   f. apple

4. g. whole grain granola

    h. crispy rice cereal bar

Name/Date _____

Empty Calories? 3

Fill in the blanks to replace empty calories.

1. Instead of cooking with butter or lard, substitute _____ _____ .

2. Instead of sweetening with sugar, substitute _____ .

Name/Date _____

Empty Calories? 4

Drinking empty calories?
Guess the teaspoons of sugar in one serving of:

1. can of soda   _____

2. apple cider   _____

3. milk shake   _____

4. cup of cocoa   _____

Name/Date _____

Empty Calories? 5

How many teaspoons of sugar do you think are in these empty calorie treats?

1. Ice cream bar

    _____

2. chocolate bar

    _____

3. cake doughnut

    _____

Nutrition and Exercise Warm-ups: Vitamin Supplements

Name/Date _____

Vitamin Supplements 1

Do a little research on vitamin absorption and decide if you think it is wise to take a vitamin supplement or not.

Circle the correct answer.

Vitamins are absorbed:

   a. the same way in food or as pills.

   b. differently in food and as pills.

   c. depends on the supplement.

Name/Date _____

Vitamin Supplements 2

Is it a good idea to eat junk food and just take vitamins to compensate? Why or why not?

_____
_____
_____
_____
_____

Name/Date _____

Vitamin Supplements 3

1. What type of vitamin should you take every day?

   _____

2. Can you take too many vitamins? Is it dangerous?

   _____
   _____
   _____

Name/Date _____

Vitamin Supplements 4

Where does your body store water-soluble and fat-soluble vitamins?

_____
_____
_____
_____

Name/Date _____

Vitamin Supplements 5

1. What type of illness is associated with the lack of vitamin C? _____

2. Historically, people doing what type of work were especially prone to this disease, and why?

   _____
   _____

3. After it was discovered that eating citrus fruits would solve the problem, what became the nickname of Britons involved in this occupation? _____

Nutrition and Exercise Warm-ups: Hydration

Name/Date _____

Hydration 1

Hunger often masks dehydration. When you think you are hungry, drink a glass of water first and then wait about ten minutes. You may find that what you actually needed was water.

Do you know some of the signs of dehydration? Place a check mark beside the signs of dehydration.

____ a. dry mouth   ____ b. extreme focus

____ c. skin stays "tented" when pinched and released   ____ d. smooth skin

____ e. salivating   ____ f. confusion   ____ g. light-headed

____ h. excessive urination   ____ i. feeling hungry

Name/Date _____

Hydration 2

Complete the sentence with the letters of the best answers from the list.

a. reduce   **b. increase**
c. maintain   **d. improve**

Good hydration helps:

1. ____ stamina.
2. ____ risk of chronic disease.
3. ____ attention and concentration.
4. ____ a healthy weight.

Name/Date _____

Hydration 3

Circle all the liquids that count toward your daily fluid intake.

a. Just water

b. Water and soda.

c. Water, milk, soda

d. Water and soup

e. Clear liquids

f. All liquids

Name/Date _____

Hydration 4

1. How much water should you try to drink each day? _____

2. Should you drink more or less water when exerting yourself? Why? _____

_____

_____

_____

Name/Date _____

Hydration 5

Mark each statement with "T" for true or "F" for false about caffeinated beverages.

1. ____ Coffee contains the highest levels of caffeine.

2. ____ Caffeine can have positive effects.

3. ____ Caffeine can cause anxiety.

4. ____ Caffeine can cause your heart to race.

5. ____ There are no side effects if you stop drinking caffeine.

Nutrition and Exercise Warm-ups: Body Mass Index

*Refer to Body Mass Index information and chart on Appendix page 40.

Name/Date _____

Body Mass Index 1

What is the lowest weight that puts a 5' tall kid into a healthy range BMI between 19 and 25?

_____

Name/Date _____

Body Mass Index 2

What is the most a 5'3" kid could weigh and stay within the healthy BMI range of 19–25?

_____

Name/Date _____

Body Mass Index 3

Just for fun, figure this one out:

If someone was 4'4" tall and had a BMI of 30, how tall would they need to be for their weight to fall within the healthy range between 19 and 25?

_____

Name/Date _____

Body Mass Index 4

What is the complete range of weight for a healthy BMI for a person who is 5'4" tall?

_____

Name/Date _____

Body Mass Index 5

What are some reasons why there are separate scales for adults and children/adolescents under 20 years of age?

_____

_____

_____

_____

Nutrition and Exercise Warm-ups: Metabolism

Name/Date _____

Metabolism 1

Joe and his twin Jerry always eat the same meals in the same portions. But Joe works out regularly and Jerry prefers to sit at the computer or read. Over time, how will their bodies differ? Why?

_____

_____

_____

Name/Date _____

Metabolism 2

Sometimes people use their metabolism as an excuse for being overweight: "I was born with a slow metabolism." What do you think; true, not true, or in between?

_____

_____

_____

Name/Date _____

Metabolism 3

If you take in more calories than you burn, the extra energy is stored through a process called

_____ .

Name/Date _____

Metabolism 4

What process does the body use to free stored energy?

_____

Name/Date _____

Metabolism 5

Can you "speed up" your metabolism? How?

_____

_____

_____

_____

Nutrition and Exercise Warm-ups: The Hunger Scale

*Refer to the Hunger Scale on Appendix page 41.

Name/Date _____

The Hunger Scale 1

Look over the Hunger Scale.

Within which range of numbers should you try to stay?

_____

Name/Date _____

The Hunger Scale 2

Practice using the Scale yourself. Track your hunger at various times.

1. At 7 A.M., I usually feel at #_____.
2. At _____ o'clock, I'm usually at #4.
3. At _____ o'clock, I'm usually at #3.
4. At 4 P.M., I'm usually at #_____.
5. At 8 P.M., I'm usually at #_____.

Name/Date _____

The Hunger Scale 3

Have the Hunger Scale and paper and pencil with you. Wait to eat until you are between #3 and #4. Divide your meal in half, and eat one half. Set your fork down. Wait a few minutes, and then jot down what number applies to your hunger. If you are at #5, stop eating. If you are still a little hungry, eat a bit more, and stop at #6 when you feel full.

1. What number represents how you felt when you stopped to rest? _____
2. What number represents how you felt when you first finished eating? _____
3. What number represents how you felt twenty minutes after eating? _____

Name/Date _____

The Hunger Scale 4

On your own paper, rewrite the Hunger Scale using your own words.

Name/Date _____

The Hunger Scale 5

On your own paper, draw a picture that represents the Hunger Scale.

Some ideas:
- a gas fuel gauge like a car has; mark it to represent the hunger scale
- balloons inflated to represent the various stages of the hunger scale

Can you think of other ideas?

Nutrition and Exercise Warm-ups:
Recognizing Hunger Signals

Name/Date _____

_____

Recognizing Hunger Signals 1

How do you know if you are really hungry? Wait 10 minutes after you start thinking you are hungry. If it is only some other feeling masquerading as hunger, the hunger sensations will usually pass. If you are still hungry after 10 minutes, eat a healthy snack.

Are you really hungry? Which of the following can masquerade as hunger? Check all that apply.

a. _____ nervousness

b. _____ vitamin deficiency

c. _____ thirst

d. _____ boredom

e. _____ all of the above

Name/Date _____

Recognizing Hunger Signals 2

On average, eating every _____ hours will keep blood sugar levels from dropping drastically.

Name/Date _____

Recognizing Hunger Signals 3

What does real hunger feel like?

_____

_____

_____

Name/Date _____

Recognizing Hunger Signals 4

How long does it take your mind to get the "full" signal from your body?

_____

Name/Date _____

Recognizing Hunger Signals 5

When should you stop eating? Should you eat until you feel "stuffed?"

_____

_____

Nutrition and Exercise Warm-ups: Selecting Healthy Foods

Name/Date _____

Selecting Healthy Foods 1

Fresh, canning, or freezing?

1. _____
   preserves foods for long periods of time.

2. _____ vegetables pre-serves the color and texture better than canning.

3 _____ vegetables are at the peak of their nutritional value.

Name/Date _____

Selecting Healthy Foods 2

What does it mean if a food is "organic"?

_____

_____

_____

_____

Name/Date _____

Selecting Healthy Foods 3

What is the maximum fat content a food may have to be labeled "low fat"? Check the correct percentage.

1. _____ 10%
2. _____ 1%
3. _____ 3%
4. _____ 6%
5. _____ 12%

Name/Date _____

Selecting Healthy Foods 4

Where can you find information on the nutritional value and ingredients of many foods? Why is this important?

_____

_____

_____

_____

Name/Date _____

Selecting Healthy Foods 5

Make a shopping list using foods from all six categories from the Food Pyramid. Be sure to account for animal and vegetable sources of protein, calcium, and healthy fats.

1. animal sources of protein: _____
2. vegetable sources of protein: _____
3. animal sources of calcium: _____
4. vegetable sources of calcium: _____
5. animal sources of healthy fats: _____
6. vegetable sources of healthy fats: _____

Nutrition and Exercise Warm-ups: Labels

*Refer to the Labels on Appendix page 42.

Name/Date _____

Labels 1

You are shopping for granola bars. Study the two labels and answer the questions.

1. How many servings do these packages

    contain? _____ servings.

What is the weight of each serving?

2. Bar A _____

3. Bar B _____

Name/Date _____

Labels 2

Compare the first 5 ingredients on the labels.

1. Which one uses more whole grains?
    _____ A   _____ B

2. Which lists more sources of sugars?
    _____ A   _____ B

3. Which product provides more protein?
    _____ A   _____ B

Name/Date _____

Labels 3

Fill in the blanks using the labels.

A single serving has:	Bar A	Bar B
1. calories	_____	_____
2. calories from fat	_____	_____
3. grams of fat	_____	_____
4. grams of sugars	_____	_____
5. grams of fiber	_____	_____
6. grams of protein	_____	_____

Name/Date _____

Labels 4

Is there any information that might be important to someone with food allergies? Where is it located?

_____

_____

_____

_____

Name/Date _____

Labels 5

Based on the information on the labels, which product would you choose? Explain why.

_____

_____

_____

_____

Nutrition and Exercise Warm-ups: Hide and Seek

Name/Date _____

Hide and Seek 1

Can you identify the common ingredient these names all signify?

beet, brown, cane, corn syrup, dextrose, fructose, glucose, galactose, honey, high-fructose corn syrup, isomalt, lactose, laevulose, maltodextrin, maltose, maple syrup, molasses, sorghum

_____

Name/Date _____

Hide and Seek 2

Can you identify the common ingredient these names all signify?

butter, coconut, hydrogenated, lard, margarine, palm kernel, partially hydrogenated, olive, poly unsaturated, shortening, soybean, trans, vegetable

_____

Name/Date _____

Hide and Seek 3

1. The key phrase to look for to identify sources of trans fats is _____ _____ _____.

2. Avoid _____ because they are high in LDL.

Name/Date _____

Hide and Seek 4

1. Can you identify the common ingredient these names all signify?

   baking soda, monosodium glutamate (MSG), sea, sodium

   _____

2. Foods described as pickled, cured, or injected with broth may have high levels of _____.

Name/Date _____

Hide and Seek 5

Once associated mostly with Chinese food, this substance has made its way into hundreds of foods. Small amounts are thought to be safe, but many people are allergic to it. It will appear on the label when it is a "stand alone" ingredient, and not mixed in with other ingredients. You may be ingesting far more than you realize as it is often added to other ingredients such as:

natural flavoring, spices, yeast extract, soy protein extract, hydrolyzed vegetable protein, texturized protein, hydrolyzed plant protein, caseinate, yeast extract, calcium caseinate, sodium caseinate, hydrolyzed corn gluten, autolyzed yeast, torula yeast.

Can you guess what it is? _____

Nutrition and Exercise Warm-ups: Healthy Cooking Practices

Name/Date _____

Healthy Cooking Practices 1

Can you match each method of cooking?

1. ____ cook quickly in a shallow pan or on a hot flat surface
2. ____ frying in a small amount of fat
3. ____ cook food by submerging it in hot oil
4. ____ cook under a hot flame
5. ____ place in a hot oven
6. ____ cook by placing food in front of a fire
7. ____ cook over boiling water
8. ____ cook by passing high frequency radio waves through food

a. deep fry
b. microwave
c. roast
d. saute
e. fry
f. steaming
g. bake
h. broil

Name/Date _____

Healthy Cooking Practices 2

A heart-healthy diet suggests cutting back on fats and oils as much as possible. Can you name three methods of cooking that are healthier for your heart?

1. _____
2. _____
3. _____

Name/Date _____

Healthy Cooking Practices 3

How many healthier substitutes for the following items can you think of to use in recipes? Use your own paper.

1. sugar
2. margarine or butter
3. mayonnaise or salad dressings
4. white flour

Can you think of healthier substitutes for other ingredients?

Name/Date _____

Healthy Cooking Practices 4

Fill in the blanks.

Cooking vegetables can deplete _____ and _____.

Cook meats _____ to kill off any _____. Keep dairy products _____ to prevent bacterial growth.

Name/Date _____

Healthy Cooking Practices 5

Rate each meal for balanced, healthy choices.

1. ____ steak, salad, whole wheat roll, and an ice cream sundae
2. ____ cheeseburger, corn, and a chocolate milk shake
3. ____ fried chicken, buttered corn bread, French fries, and cake
4. ____ baked fish, carrots and peas, brown rice, and berries with non-fat yogurt

a. Good
b. Better
c. Best
d. Not Even Close.

Nutrition and Exercise Warm-ups: Diet Myths, Alternatives, & Choices

---

Name/Date _____

Diet Myths, Alternatives, & Choices 1

Mark "T" for True or "F" for False.

1. ____ An apple a day keeps the doctor away.
2. ____ Limes cure scurvy.
3. ____ Eating carrots is good for your eyes.
4. ____ Drinking ice-cold water helps you lose weight.
5. ____ A glass of warm milk will help you fall asleep.

Name/Date _____

Diet Myths, Alternatives, & Choices 2

What is a vegetarian? Vegetarians do not eat meat. Some vegetarians, known as ovo-lacto vegetarians, also consume dairy products such as milk, eggs, and cheese. Other vegetarians, known as vegans, only eat plant-based foods.

On your own paper, write a meal plan for a vegetarian diet. Specify if it is an ovo-lacto meal or a vegan meal.

Name/Date _____

Diet Myths, Alternatives, & Choices 3

Eating locally grown food is a great way to get the freshest foods possible while using less gas for transportation. If you lived in the following regions, what would you eat most? Look up the diets of people native to these areas and see what they eat.

1. A tropical region _____

2. A forest region _____

3. A desert region _____

4. An arctic region _____

Name/Date _____

Diet Myths, Alternatives, & Choices 4

What is a macrobiotic diet?

_____

_____

_____

_____

MACROBIOTICS

Name/Date _____

Diet Myths, Alternatives, & Choices 5

The right foods can make us feel better. Name a food that can help the following conditions.

1. the common cold _____

2. anemia _____

3. rickets _____

Nutrition and Exercise Warm-ups: On the Road

Name/Date _____

On the Road 1

The convenience store is full of unhealthy food. What are some things you should pack to help make the most out of your road trip?

_____
_____
_____
_____

Name/Date _____

On the Road 2

Traveling is a great way to try new foods. On your own paper, list a healthy new food to try if you visited each of these states.

1. Maine
2. Louisiana
3. Maryland
4. Wyoming
5. New Mexico
6. Washington

Taos ☆

New Mexico

Name/Date _____

On the Road 3

It's time for a picnic! Pack a healthy picnic basket based on the food pyramid.

Fruits _____
Vegetables _____
Grains _____
Dairy _____
Meat and Beans _____
Beverages _____

Name/Date _____

On the Road 4

At the family reunion, Aunt May brings you a huge slice of her famous chocolate pie. You know this dessert is bad for you, but when you say "No thanks," Aunt May cries in a hurt tone, "But I made it just for you!" What would you do?

1. ____ Eat the pie to make her happy.
2. ____ Take the pie and eat a bite or two.
3. ____ Tell her you're full, but promise to take a piece home for later.

Name/Date _____

On the Road 5

Estimate the calories and grams of fat for your Thanksgiving meal at Grandma's on your own paper. How much is the total meal? If you wanted to eat healthier, what would you eat more of? Less of?

1. 3 oz. of roast turkey, no skin
2. 1/2 c. gravy
3. 1/2 c. corn bread stuffing
4. 1/2 c. cranberry sauce
5. 1/2 c. mashed potatoes
6. 1/2 c. candied sweet potatoes
7. 1/2 c. green bean casserole
8. 2 sweet pickles and 10 olives
9. 1 piece cream cheese stuffed celery
10. 1/2 c. buttered peas
11. 1 roll with butter
12. 1 piece pumpkin pie with whipped cream

Nutrition and Exercise Warm-ups: Restaurants

Name/Date _____

Restaurants 1

List the calories and grams of fat for each fast food item. What is the healthiest thing to eat?

McDonald's™

1. Big Mac™ _____
2. super-sized french fries _____
3. value fries _____
4. chocolate shake (12 oz.) _____
5. side salad _____
6. chicken McNuggets™ (6 pieces) _____

Subway™

7. roast beef sub (6") _____
8. cheese steak _____

Dunkin Donuts™

9. éclair _____
10. chocolate chip muffin _____

Name/Date _____

Restaurants 2

Mark "T" for True or "F" for False for these buffet questions.

1. ____ The phrase "All you can eat" is a challenge.
2. ____ Unless you get four or five plates full, you have wasted your money.
3. ____ Starting with a salad and some soup is a smart thing to do.
4. ____ Try new foods when you see them.

Name/Date _____

Restaurants 3

Whoever said variety is the spice of life must have been thinking of ethnic restaurants. Using a phone book, look up the different kinds of ethnic food available in your town. Which ones have you tried?

_____

_____

_____

Name/Date _____

Restaurants 4

If you wanted to eat healthy when eating out, what would be the best foods to order at each of these style of restaurants? Answer on your own paper.

Mexican
Pizza
Seafood

Chinese
Barbecue
Italian

Name/Date _____

Restaurants 5

Salad bars are popular in many restaurants. What would you choose from the list below for a healthy, filling meal? Circle your choices.

iceberg lettuce	spring mix greens	olives
bacon bits	French dressing	croutons
Italian dressing	ranch dressing	peppers
garbanzo beans	hard-boiled eggs	onions
cherry tomatoes	shredded cheese	cucumbers

Nutrition and Exercise Warm-ups: Overeating

Name/Date _____

Overeating 1

Eating can be a comforting reaction to emotional stressors. Which of these emotions might influence someone to overeat?

a. nervous

b. impulsive

c. scared

d. hopeless

e. feeling trapped

f. depression

g. angry

h. frustrated

i. feeling confused or conflicted

j. competitive

k. disappointment

l. overwhelmed

When you feel like overeating, don't ask "What can I eat?" but ask "What's eating me?"

Name/Date _____

Overeating 2

When it seems like there is nothing to do, eating becomes a way to kill time. But you can beat boredom!
Get creative and write a short paragraph on your own paper about beating boredom without overeating.

Name/Date _____

Overeating 3

Did you realize that most people eat the same five or six meals every week? If you regularly eat fatty or sugary foods, this habitual eating pattern can add unwanted pounds.

On your own paper, list foods you eat out of habit. Then think of some new foods you'd like to try. Keep your list in mind the next time you're at the grocery store!

Name/Date _____

Overeating 4

Whether it's your birthday cake or Grandma's special Christmas cookies, there are times when everyone should indulge, just a little bit. Can you figure out the two-word key to enjoying special treats?

_____ _____

Name/Date _____

Overeating 5

Some people feel that their weight is beyond their control, and nothing they can do will change how fat they feel. This attitude is another way of saying "I give up." On your own paper, write a list of excuses some people might use to give up, and then come up with reasons why those excuses are just that—excuses.

Nutrition and Exercise Warm-ups: Change Your Behavior

Name/Date _____

Change Your Behavior 1

Got an A on the big test? Beat your personal best time? Some people might reward themselves  with desserts, but this kind of reward isn't good for you. On your own paper, think up some other ways to celebrate a milestone that don't involve food.

Name/Date _____

Change Your Behavior 2

Are any of these habits you need to change? On your own paper, write down how you can make positive changes.

1. ____ Eat quickly, gulp down food.
2. ____ Eat in front of the television.
3. ____ Snack all day long until bedtime.
4. ____ Use sugary or caffeinated foods and drinks to get a quick energy lift.
5. ____ Don't get enough exercise.

Name/Date _____

Change Your Behavior 3

What you don't know can hurt you! Knowledge allows you to make better choices. Do you know:

1. ____ your BMI percentile?
2. ____ how many calories you need?
3. ____ what's in the foods you eat?
4. ____ how to read labels for nutritional information?
5. ____ how much exercise you need each week?

Name/Date _____

Change Your Behavior 4

Trying new things can lead to healthier eating. What are you willing to do this week? Check those that apply, and on your own paper, make a plan—a grocery list, the name of a cookbook, etc.—to do it!

____ Try a new food.
____ Cook a new recipe.
____ Make a shopping list of healthy foods.
____ Try a dish from another culture.

Name/Date _____

Change Your Behavior 5

How long does it take to learn a new behavior or habit? Circle the correct choice.

a. 5 days   b. 11 days

c. 18 days   d. 21 days

e. 26 days

How long should you stick with a new exercise plan to make sure it becomes a habit? _____

Nutrition and Exercise Warm-ups: Dieting Disasters

Name/Date _____

Dieting Disasters 1

Can you identify why this fad diet is disastrous? List all the reasons below.

_____
_____
_____
_____

On the Miracle Beverly Hills Diet, you eat just 400 calories a day and the weight flies off! No need to exercise!

Name/Date _____

Dieting Disasters 2

Can you identify why this fad diet is disastrous?

_____
_____
_____
_____
_____

Want to lose weight? Stop eating fattening vegetables! By giving up vegetables, the weight will fall off!

Name/Date _____

Dieting Disasters 3

Can you identify why this fad diet is disastrous?

_____
_____
_____
_____

New! The amazing Houdini all-natural herbal supplement will peel off pounds with no harmful side effects!

Buy it today!

HOUDINI
Pounds Disappear!

Name/Date _____

Dieting Disasters 4

Can you identify why this fad diet is disastrous?

_____
_____
_____
_____

The All-Grape Diet WILL work for you! Eat nothing but grapes for three weeks and lose up to twenty pounds!

Name/Date _____

Dieting Disasters 5

Can you identify why this fad is disastrous?

_____
_____
_____
_____

LOW HIGH

Tired of working out? The new Saddlebag Shaker works out for you! Just relax, and the pounds will melt off!

Nutrition and Exercise Warm-ups: Dieting Wonder Drugs?

Name/Date _____

Dieting Wonder Drugs? 1

What is the difference between an FDA-approved drug and a dietary supplement?

_____

_____

_____

_____

Name/Date _____

Dieting Wonder Drugs? 2

What is the FDA? What does it do? Why does it treat drugs differently than supplements?

_____

_____

_____

_____

Name/Date _____

Dieting Wonder Drugs? 3

In 1992, the FDA recalled diet products containing guar gum.

The claim: Guar gum swells in the stomach so you feel full and eat less.

The reality: Guar gum caused swelling and blockages in the throat, stomach, and intestines, resulting in numerous hospitalizations and emergency surgeries.

What do nutritionists recommend eating instead of guar gum to feel fuller and eat less? Unscramble the letters to find out.

B I F R E

_____

Name/Date _____

Dieting Wonder Drugs? 4

In the late 1990s, an alarming number of young people were hospitalized for heart problems that were linked to using a diet drug known as Fen-phen. The FDA banned products containing this and other similar chemical ingredients. Using the internet and your own paper, research some of the problems Fen-phen caused. Do you think the FDA did the right thing in banning the drug?

Name/Date _____

Dieting Wonder Drugs? 5

Mark "T" for True or "F" for false.

1. ____ The FDA banned the diet supplement ephedra in 2003.

2. ____ Over 16,000 adverse reactions had been associated with the supplement.

3. ____ Ephedra is also called Ma Huang.

4. ____ Common side effects include tremors, heart palpitations, and insomnia.

Nutrition and Exercise Warm-ups: Allergies & Health Issues

Name/Date _____

Allergies & Health Issues 1

Two million kids in the United States have food allergies. Eating even a very small amount of a food a person is allergic to can make them very sick. An allergic reaction may be immediate and severe, or it may happen over the next few hours. Would you recognize the signs of food allergies? List as many possible allergic reactions as possible on the lines below.

_____

_____

_____

Name/Date _____

Allergies & Health Issues 2

Unscramble these common food allergies.

1. rcno _____
2. thawe _____
3. gseg _____
4. neyosabs _____
5. scwo kiml _____
6. tupesna _____
7. hlisfsleh _____

Name/Date _____

Allergies & Health Issues 3

What is an anaphylactic shock?

_____

_____

_____

_____

_____

_____

Name/Date _____

Allergies & Health Issues 4

If you developed diabetes, how would you have to change your diet and lifestyle?

_____

_____

_____

Name/Date _____

Allergies & Health Issues 5

How can diet affect your cholesterol or blood pressure? What changes can you make that will positively impact your health?

_____

_____

_____

Nutrition and Exercise Warm-ups: Fitness Facts

Name/Date _____

Fitness Facts 1

Are we an overweight, under-exercised nation?
Mark "T" for True or "F" for False.

1. _____ Lack of exercise does not significantly raise the risk of chronic disease.
2. _____ Over 67% of the adult population in the United States is overweight or obese.*
3. _____ The number of overweight children has tripled since 1980.
4. _____ 20% of adults do not get enough exercise.
5. _____ Only 28% of 9th through 12th graders exercise for 30 minutes a day 5 days a week.

*defined as a BMI over 25

Name/Date _____

Fitness Facts 2

How many calories would a 125-lb. person burn doing 20 minutes of:

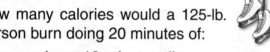

1. running a 12-minute mile _____
2. walking moderately fast _____
3. skating (ice or roller) _____
4. riding a bike (leisurely) _____
5. Frisbee (casual) _____
6. volleyball (casual) _____

Name/Date _____

Fitness Facts 3

Circle the correct choice.

Young people are becoming heavier because:

a. They are larger than their ancestors.

b. They have more good food available to them than 20 years ago.

c. They are becoming more sedentary.

Name/Date _____

Fitness Facts 4

What is a healthy weight loss for middle-school age children? Circle the correct choice(s).

1. 10 pounds a year
2. 1 pound a week
3. 1 pound a month
4. 2 pounds a month
5. as much as possible

Name/Date _____

Fitness Facts 5

Fill in the blank with the correct choice.

Physically inactive people are _____ as likely to develop coronary heat disease as people who exercise moderately.

a. four times   b. not
c. just   d. twice
e. ten times

Nutrition and Exercise Warm-ups: Do You Know?

Name/Date _____

Do You Know? 1

Define the following words.

calorie: _____

_____

calorie count: _____

_____

Name/Date _____

Do You Know? 2

What is the basic formula for weight loss?

_____

_____

_____

_____

Name/Date _____

| helmet | loose | layers |
| shoes | evaporation | |

Do You Know? 3

Do you know what to wear when exercising? Fill in the blanks with the right word.

1. When exercising in hot weather, wear _____ clothing.
2. When exercising in cold weather, wear _____ of clothing.
3. Wear _____ with good support and cushioning for the type of exercise or sport you are doing.
4. ALWAYS protect your head with a _____ when biking or blading.
5. Never wear rubberized or plastic clothing, as it prevents the _____ of sweat, which is how your body keeps from becoming overheated.

Name/Date _____

Do You Know? 4

Fill in the blanks with the correct body parts.

1. Weight training develops stronger _____ and _____.
2. Aerobic exercise strengthens your _____ and _____.
3. Low-impact exercises put less stress on your _____.

Name/Date _____

Do You Know? 5

Can you guess the best way to protect yourself?

1. Protect your eyes with _____.
2. Protect your mouth and teeth with a _____.
3. Protect knees and elbows with _____.
4. Protect your shins with _____.

Nutrition and Exercise Warm-ups: Fitness for the Heart

Name/Date _____

Fitness for the Heart 1

How does aerobic exercise benefit your heart?

_____
_____
_____
_____

Name/Date _____

Fitness for the Heart 2

3	30
20	5
week	

Fill in the blanks with the choices from the word bank.

The recommended schedule for doing aerobic exercise is _____ to _____ times per _____ for at least _____ to _____ minutes.

Name/Date _____

Fitness for the Heart 3

Is aerobic exercise the only kind of exercise that benefits your heart? What other kinds of exercises are good for your heart?

_____
_____
_____
_____

Name/Date _____

Fitness for the Heart 4

Do you know how to find your heart rate? Follow these instructions!
1. Before you begin any activity, take your pulse. Count your pulse for 10 seconds and multiply by 6 to find your resting heart rate.
2. Do at least five minutes of aerobic activity.
3. Take your pulse rate again within 5 seconds of finishing your activity, because your pulse rate drops quickly.
4. What is your active heart rate? _____

Name/Date _____

Fitness for the Heart 5

Fill in the blanks.

A typical workout includes time to warm up, be active, and time to cool down. Answer these questions about a good middle-school workout.
1. Middle-school age kids need _____ to _____ minutes a day of activity at least _____ days a week.
2. Warm up: _____ to _____ minutes
3. Activity: _____ to _____ minutes
4. Cool down period: _____ to _____ minutes

Nutrition and Exercise Warm-ups:
The Benefits of Exercise

Use the following words to fill in the blanks. Some words may be used more than once.

exercise	chemicals	protects
lessons	metabolism	diabetes
calorie	stress	difficulty
brain	manage	chronic
restful	anxiety	lowers
calming	release	muscles
sleep	commitment	pressure
weight	denser	socialize
dopamine	climbing	cholesterol

Name/Date _____

The Benefits of Exercise 1

Fill in the blanks from the word bank.

Exercise relieves _____.
Exercising stimulates healthy
_____ in
your _____. The
release of _____ during
exercise has a _____
effect. Exercise reduces the symptoms of
_____ and depression.

Name/Date _____

The Benefits of Exercise 2

Fill in the blanks from the word bank.

Exercise combats _____
diseases. Exercise builds a stronger heart
and _____ bones,
lowers blood _____,
boosts good _____
(HDL), _____ bad
cholesterol (LDL), and _____
against many types of cancer.

Name/Date _____

The Benefits of Exercise 3

Fill in the blanks from the word bank.

Exercise helps you to _____
your _____. Exercise
increases your _____, so
the _____-burning benefits
continue even after you stop. Managing
your weight with _____
will also help cut the chances of developing
_____.

Name/Date _____

The Benefits of Exercise 4

Fill in the blanks from the word bank.

Exercise helps you _____
better. People who have _____
falling asleep often find it helpful to
_____ late in the day. The
_____ of stress, coupled
with slightly tired _____,
promotes more _____ sleep.

Name/Date _____

The Benefits of Exercise 5

Fill in the blanks from the word bank.

Exercise is a great way to _____.
People who exercise with a friend tend to stick
to their _____ longer than
people who exercise alone. Go hiking or rock
_____ with a group. Take
tennis or golf _____, and
meet other people with similar interests.

Nutrition and Exercise Warm-ups: Journaling

Name/Date _____

Journaling 1

On your own paper, start an exercise journal. For the first day, create the basic activity page that lists the day of the week, the activity, and how long you exercised. Remember, all types of activities count, including walking, playing, doing chores, and playing sports. How much activity did you get today?

Name/Date _____

Journaling 2

Add a food page to your journal. Start by tracking every single thing you eat and drink. Important things to note include: how many fruits did you eat? How many servings of vegetables did you eat? Did you drink enough water? Did you take a vitamin? Are there areas of your diet where you can improve your choices?

Name/Date _____

Journaling 3

Make a page for your journal to help you measure the difference between muscle and fat. Add columns for your waist, hips, thighs, and arms. Measure each part with a tape measure once a week. Is there a relationship between the circumference of your body and your physical fitness?

Name/Date _____

Journaling 4

Challenge yourself! Make a new page for your journal that lists the new activities and foods you are going to try. Will you bike to the park? Try Thai food? Sign up for a new dance class? Eat brown rice? How will you achieve your new goals?

Name/Date _____

Journaling 5

Add a motivational rewards page to your journal. What things will motivate you to keep moving and eating healthy? Make these tangible, attainable rewards. Rewards can be something big like a manicure or a new MP3 player, or something free, like looking better in your clothes or finishing a 5K race.

Nutrition and Exercise Warm-ups: Appendix 1: The Food Pyramid

Name: _____ Date: _____

List a few foods in each group from the new food pyramid that you enjoy.

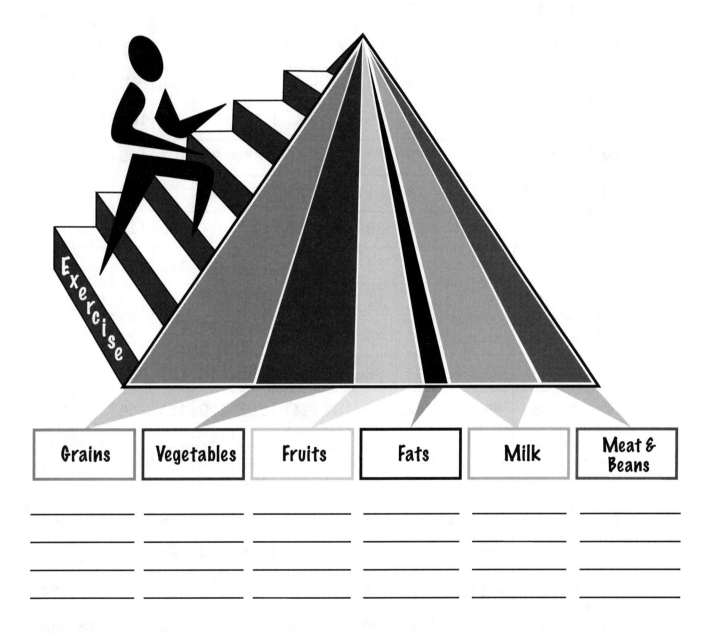

Grains	Vegetables	Fruits	Fats	Milk	Meat & Beans
_____	_____	_____	_____	_____	_____
_____	_____	_____	_____	_____	_____
_____	_____	_____	_____	_____	_____
_____	_____	_____	_____	_____	_____

Was it harder to think of favorite foods in some categories? Brainstorm as a class and discuss healthy ways to prepare foods that might encourage you to eat them more often.

Nutrition and Exercise Warm-ups:
Appendix 2: Adolescent Body Mass Index Chart

Body Mass Index, or BMI, is the measurement of body mass, which takes into consideration a person's height and weight. Keeping your weight within normal ranges is a good goal to include as you develop a healthy lifestyle.

BMI Number

Height (inches)	16	19	20	21	22	23	24	25	26	27	30	31	32	33
46	48	57	60	63	66	69	72	75	78	81	90	93	96	99
47	50	59	62	65	69	72	75	78	81	84	94	97	100	103
48	52	62	65	68	72	75	78	81	85	88	98	101	104	108
49	54	64	68	71	75	78	81	85	88	92	102	105	109	112
50	56	67	71	74	78	81	85	88	92	96	106	110	113	117
51	59	70	73	77	81	85	88	92	96	99	110	114	118	122
52	61	73	76	80	84	88	92	96	100	103	115	119	123	126
53	63	75	79	83	87	91	95	99	103	107	119	123	127	131
54	66	78	82	87	91	95	99	103	107	111	124	128	132	136
55	68	81	86	90	94	98	103	107	111	116	129	133	137	141
56	71	84	89	93	98	102	107	111	115	120	133	138	142	147
57	73	87	92	97	101	106	110	115	120	124	138	143	147	152
58	76	90	95	100	105	110	114	119	124	129	143	148	153	157
59	79	94	99	103	108	113	118	123	128	133	148	153	158	163
60	81	97	102	107	112	117	122	128	133	138	153	158	163	168
61	84	100	105	111	116	121	127	132	137	142	158	164	169	174
62	87	103	109	114	120	125	131	136	142	147	164	169	174	180
63	84	107	112	118	124	129	135	141	146	152	169	175	180	185
64	93	110	116	122	128	134	139	145	151	157	174	180	186	192

Weight (pounds)

Nutrition and Exercise Warm-ups:
Appendix 3: The Hunger Scale

Beyond Hungry 1
so hungry you can't think; may
feel light-headed, uncoordinated,
nauseous, out of touch; may not even
feel hungry anymore

2 **Very Hungry/Ravenous**
stomach rumbles; may feel irritable, have
a headache; too hungry to stay focused
on tasks; coordination wanes

Motivated To Eat Now 3
thoughts focused on getting food;
stomach rumbles; may feel empty;
concentration wanes

4 **Aware Of Hunger**
may feel a little hungry, but can wait if you
have to

Almost Satisfied 5
you have eaten enough to replenish
your body; your brain is just beginning
to feel satisfied

6 **Satisfied, Comfortably Full**
your brain says "we're full, stop eating
now;" you feel satisfied

Very Full 7
past the point of satisfaction; may think
"It tastes so good, just a few more
bites."

8 **Overly Full**
uncomfortably full; may think "I should
have stopped sooner."

Extremely Full, Stuffed 9
may feel really uncomfortable or
bloated; may want to loosen clothes
or withdraw from social activities; may
want to nap

10 **Beyond Full**
may feel physically miserable or
nauseous; be barely able to move, may
think "I never want to look at food again."

Nutrition and Exercise Warm-ups:
Appendix 4: Labels

A

Nutritional Facts

Serving Size 1 bar (33g)
Servings Per Container 6

Amount Per Serving

Calories 120   Calories from Fat 20

	% Daily Value*
Total Fat 2g	3%
Saturated Fat 0.5g	3%
Trans Fat 0g	
Cholesterol 0mg	0%
Sodium 90mg	4%
Total Carbohydrate 24g	8%
Dietary Fiber 1g	4%
Sugars 11g	
Protein 2g	

Vitamin A 0%	•	Vitamin C 0%
Calcium 2%	•	Iron 4%

*Percent Daily Values are based on a 2,000 calorie diet. Your daily values may be higher or lower depending on your calorie needs:

		Calories:	2,000	2,500
Total Fat	Less than		65g	80g
Saturated Fat	Less than		20g	25g
Cholesterol	Less than		300mg	300mg
Sodium	Less than		2,400mg	2,400mg
Total Carbohydrate			300g	375g
Dietary Fiber			25g	30g

INGREDIENTS: ROLLED OATS, CRISP RICE (RICE FLOUR, SUGAR, BARLEY MALT EXTRACT, SALT), WHEAT FLAKES, BROWN SUGAR, WHEY POWDER, SOYBEAN OIL, HONEY, MOLASSES, BROWN RICE SYRUP, EVAPORATED CANE JUICE, RASPBERRY FLAVORED FRUIT PIECES (SUGAR, CRANBERRIES, CITRIC ACID, NATURAL RASPBERRY FLAVOR WITH OTHER NATURAL FLAVORS, ELDERBERRY JUICE CONCENTRATE, SUNFLOWER OIL), RASPBERRY JUICE CONCENTRATE, WHEY PROTEIN CONCENTRATE, SOY LECITHIN, NATURAL FLAVORS, RED BEET POWDER, SALT, SLICED ALMONDS, MALIC ACID.

CONTAINS: WHEAT, MILK, SOY, ALMONDS, GLUTEN. MANUFACTURED IN A FACILITY THAT USES PEANUTS AND OTHER TREE NUTS.

B

Nutritional Facts

Serving Size 1 bar (35g)
Servings Per Container 6

Amount Per Serving

Calories 140   Calories from Fat 45

	% Daily Value*
Total Fat 5g	8%
Saturated Fat 0.5g	3%
Trans Fat 0g	
Cholesterol 0mg	0%
Sodium 115mg	5%
Total Carbohydrate 19g	6%
Fiber 4g	15%
Soluble Fiber 1g	
Insoluble Fiber 3g	
Sugars 5g	
Protein 7g	

Vitamin A	0%	•	Vitamin C	0%
Calcium	0%	•	Iron	8%

*Percent Daily Values are based on a 2,000 calorie diet. Your daily values may be higher or lower depending on your calorie needs:

		Calories:	2,000	2,500
Total Fat	Less than		65g	80g
Sat Fat	Less than		20g	25g
Cholesterol	Less than		300mg	300mg
Sodium	Less than		2,400mg	2,400mg
Total Carbohydrate			300g	375g
Dietary Fiber			25g	30g

Calories per gram:
Fat 9   •   Carbohydrate 4   •   Protein 4

INGREDIENTS: WHOLE HARD RED WINTER WHEAT, OATS, RYE, BARLEY, TRITICALE, LONG GRAIN BROWN RICE, BUCKWHEAT, SESAME SEEDS, WHOLE ALMONDS, BROWN RICE SYRUP, SOY PROTEIN ISOLATE, SOY GRIT, EVAPORATED CANE JUICE CRYSTALS, CHICORY ROOT FIBER, WHOLE FLAX SEEDS, EVAPORATED CANE JUICE SYRUP, RICE STARCH, CORN FLOUR, HONEY, EXPELLER PRESSED CANOLA OIL, VEGETABLE GLYCERIN, OAT FIBER, EVAPORATED SALT, NATURAL FLAVORS, MOLASSES, SOY LECITHIN, PEANUT FLOUR, WHEY, ANNATTO COLOR.
CONTAINS WHEAT, ALMOND, SOY, PEANUT AND MILK INGREDIENTS. MAY CONTAIN TRACES OF OTHER TREE NUTS.

Answer Keys

Diet 1 (p. 2)
1. 5

Diet 2 (p. 2)
1. F   2. F   3. F   4. F   5. F

Diet 3 (p. 2)
Answers will vary.

Diet 4 (p. 2)
1. Yes   2. No   3. Yes
4. No   5. Yes

Diet 5 (p. 2)
1. c   2. e   3. b   4. a   5. d

Feed Your Brain 1 (p. 3)
nutrition, regulate, peak, essential

Feed Your Brain 2 (p. 3)
1. c   2. d/a   3. e   4. b   5. a

Feed Your Brain 3 (p. 3)
1. b   2. d   3. a   4. c

Feed Your Brain 4 (p. 3)
1. T   2. T   3. T   4. F

Feed Your Brain 5 (p. 3)
1. N   2. N   3. N   4. H
5. N   6. H   7. N

Exercise 1 (p. 4)
1. bones: increases density
2. joints: improves flexibility and range of motion
3. blood vessels: improves circulation; lowers blood pressure
4. brain: relieves stress; increases dopamine and serotonin
5. muscles: strengthens, improves stamina and coordination

Exercise 2 (p. 4)
1. jumping rope   2. walking
3. jogging   4. cycling
5. cross country skiing

Exercise 3 (p. 4)
b

Exercise 4 (p. 4)
c

Exercise 5 (p. 4)
525 minutes; 35 miles

Proper Rest 1 (p. 5)
a

Proper Rest 2 (p. 5)
1. d   2. a   3. b   4. c

Proper Rest 3 (p. 5)
1. T   2. F   3. T   4. F
5. T

Proper Rest 4 (p. 5)
2. and 4.
Tryptophan is a chemical in milk that helps the brain relax. It is also found in other dairy products, soy products, peanuts, and whole grains.

Proper Rest 5 (p. 5)
Answers will vary.

Grains 1 (p. 6)
Answers may include wheat, oats, rice, corn, barley, millet, buckwheat, or groats.

Grains 2 (p. 6)
1. c   2. a   3. b

Grains 3 (p. 6)
complex carbohydrates

Grains 4 (p. 6)
Check 1, 5, 6, and 8.

Grains 5 (p. 6)
Answers will vary. Answers may include:
1. pasta   2. tortillas
3. rice   4. rice
5. pita   6. matzoh
7. millet   8. oatmeal
9. bread   10. pretzels

Vegetables 1 (p. 7)
Teacher check drawing.

Vegetables 2 (p. 7)
1. potato, carrot, radish, etc.
2. celery, leeks, rhubarb
3. scallions, lettuce, spinach
4. broccoli, cauliflower
5. zucchini, cucumber, tomato
6. green beans, lentils, peanuts

Vegetables 3 (p. 7)
1. rutabaga   2. arugula
3. squash   4. endive
5. artichoke   6. kohlrabi
7. zucchini   8. cauliflower

Vegetables 4 (p. 7)
1. fiber   2. vitamins
3. minerals

Vegetables 5 (p. 7)
Nutrient-dense foods have a high nutrient/calorie ratio, meaning they are a rich source of nutrients when compared to their calorie content.

Fruits 1 (p. 8)
pumpkin

Fruits 2 (p. 8)
sugar

Fruits 3 (p. 8)
a minimum of three

Fruits 4 (p. 8)
fructose

Fruits 5 (p. 8)
Answers will vary.

Fats 1 (p. 9)
Answers will vary.

Fats 2 (p. 9)
1. saturated and unsaturated
2. Saturated fats raise blood cholesterol. Trans fats are linked to obesity, diabetes, arteriosclerosis, and heart disease.

Fats 3 (p. 9)
red meat, poultry, pork products, eggs, dairy products, hydrogenated or partially hydrogenated oils, lard

Fats 4 (p. 9)
soybeans, olives, safflower oil, sunflower oil, nuts, fatty cold-water fish, avocados

Fats 5 (p. 9)
Answers may include flax oil, safflower oil, oily fish (like tuna, salmon, and mackerel), pumpkin seeds, walnuts, and walnut oil.

Milk Products 1 (p. 10)
osteoporosis, density, fracture

Milk Products 2 (p. 10)
c

Milk Products 3 (p. 10)
soft and hard cheeses, yogurt, butter, ice cream, and others

Milk Products 4 (p. 10)
3 servings a day. Answers will vary.

Milk Products 5 (p. 10)
1. HDL and LDL
2. LDL is "bad" because it increases the risk of coronary heart disease

Meat, Beans, & Nuts 1 (p. 11)
d

Meat, Beans, & Nuts 2 (p. 11)
sodium (nitrates or preservatives are also acceptable)

Meat, Beans, & Nuts 3 (p. 11)
b

Meat, Beans, & Nuts 4 (p. 11)
Vegetarians can eat dairy products (if they are ovo-lacto vegetarians), beans, lentils, tofu, textured vegetable protein, nuts, and seeds to get protein.

Meat, Beans, & Nuts 5 (p. 11)
1. pork, beef, buffalo, venison, mutton
2. chicken, turkey, duck, ostrich
3. cod, tilapia, salmon, flounder, trout
4. tuna, sardines, mackerel, salmon
5. clams, crabs, shrimp, scallops
6. walnuts, hazelnuts, cashews, almonds
7. kidney beans, garbanzo beans, lentils, soybeans, peas

Exercise 1 (p. 12)
1. obesity
2. muscle weakness
3. lower bone density
4. heart problems

Exercise 2 (p. 12)
Exercise stimulates brain chemicals, keeps them regulated, and is helpful for symptoms of depression.

Exercise 3 (p. 12)
Exercise burns calories and boosts your metabolism.

Exercise 4 (p. 12)
False. All movement counts.

Exercise 5 (p. 12)
Answers will vary.

Serving Sizes 1 (p. 13)
b

Serving Sizes 2 (p. 13)
c

Serving Sizes 3 (p. 13)
a

Serving Sizes 4 (p. 13)
c

Serving Sizes 5 (p. 13)
d

Balanced Meals 1 (p. 14)
d

Balanced Meals 2–5 (p. 14)
Answers will vary.

Empty Calories 1 (p. 15)
whole grain cereals, whole grain breads, fresh fruits

Empty Calories? 2 (p. 15)
1. b   2. d   3. f   4. g

Empty Calories 3 (p. 15)
1. vegetable oils
2. fruit juice or applesauce

Empty Calories 4 (p. 15)
All amounts are approximate. Different brands of food vary.
1. 7 tsp.   2. 5.5 tsp.
3. 13 tsp. (reg. McDonald's shake)
4. 5 tsp.

Empty Calories 5 (p. 15)
1. 5 tsp.   2. 7–8 tsp.
3. 4–5 tsp.

Vitamin Supplements 1 (p. 16)
b

Vitamin Supplements 2 (p. 16)
No. There are many micronutrients in foods that are not simulated in supplements.

Vitamin Supplements 3 (p. 16)
1. a multivitamin
2. Yes. Fat soluble vitamins can cause organ damage in excessively high levels.

Vitamin Supplements 4 (p. 16)
Water soluble vitamins are stored briefly in the body and then excreted by the kidneys. Fat soluble vitamins are stored in the liver.

Vitamin Supplements 5 (p. 16)
1. scurvy
2. Sailors, because they had no fresh fruits with ascorbic acid to eat on long voyages.
3. Limeys

Hydration 1 (p. 17)
a, c, f, g, i should all be checked.

Hydration 2 (p. 17)
1. b   2. a   3. d   4. c

Hydration 3 (p. 17)
f

Hydration 4 (p. 17)
1. 6 to 8 glasses
2. more, because the body loses water when sweating

Hydration 5 (p. 17)
1. F   2. T   3. T   4. T   5. F

Body Mass Index 1 (p. 18)
97

Body Mass Index 2 (p. 18)
141

Body Mass Index 3 (p. 18)
57 inches, or 4 ft. 9 in

Body Mass Index 4 (p. 18)
110–145 lbs.

Body Mass Index 5 (p. 18)
Children have changing muscle and bone densities as they grow.

Metabolism 1 (p. 19)
Joe will have a higher metabolic rate and will be healthier. Jerry will have a lower metabolic rate, will be heavier, and will have increased chances of health problems.

Metabolism 2 (p. 19)
In between, because metabolic rate is partially determined by genetics, but metabolic rate can also be increased through exercise.

Metabolism 3 (p. 19)
anabolism

Metabolism 4 (p. 19)
catabolism

Metabolism 5 (p. 19)
yes, through exercising

The Hunger Scale 1 (p. 20)
between 3 and 7

The Hunger Scale 2–5 (p. 20)
Answers will vary.

Recognizing Hunger Signals 1 (p. 21)
e

Recognizing Hunger Signals 2 (p.21)
three

Recognizing Hunger Signals 3 (p.21)
Answers will vary.

Recognizing Hunger Signals 4 (p.21)
20 minutes

Recognizing Hunger Signals 5 (p.21)
Stop when you feel comfortable.

Selecting Healthy Foods 1 (p. 22)
1. Canning   2. Freezing
3. Fresh

Selecting Healthy Foods 2 (p. 22)
Organic food is grown without
pesticides or chemical fertilizers.

Selecting Healthy Foods 3 (p. 22)
3

Selecting Healthy Foods 4 (p. 22)
The label lists ingredients and
nutritional information so you can
make informed choices and compare
different brands.

Selecting Healthy Foods 5 (p. 22)
1. lean beef, chicken, fish, milk, eggs
2. nuts, tofu, beans, lentils
3. milk, cheese, yogurt
4. tofu, molasses, almonds, greens
5. salmon, cod, mackerel
6. olives, avocados, corn oil, walnut
   oil

Labels 1 (p. 23)
1. 6   2. 33 g   3. 35 g

Labels 2 (p. 23)
1. B   2. A   3. B

Labels 3 (p. 23)

	Bar A	Bar B
1.	120	140
2.	20	45
3.	2	5
4.	11	5
5.	1	4
6.	2	7

Labels 4 (p. 23)
Allergy-causing ingredients are listed
at the bottom of the labels.

Labels 5 (p. 23)
Answers will vary.

Hide and Seek 1 (p. 24)
sugar

Hide and Seek 2 (p. 24)
fat

Hide and Seek 3 (p. 24)
1. partially hydrogenated oil
2. saturated fats

Hide and Seek 4 (p. 24)
1. salt   2. sodium

Hide and Seek 5 (p. 24)
Monosodium glutamate (MSG)

Healthy Cooking Practices 1 (p.25)
1. e   2. d   3. a   4. h
5. g   6. c   7. f   8. b

Healthy Cooking Practices 2 (p.25)
Answers include broiling, steaming,
baking, poaching, or microwaving.

Healthy Cooking Practices 3 (p.25)
1. honey, fruit juice, low-calorie
   sweetener
2. healthy oils, low-fat cream
   cheese, margarine blends
3. vinaigrettes, mustards, low-
   calorie dressings
4. whole wheat, soy, and rice flours

Healthy Cooking Practices 4 (p.25)
vitamins, minerals, thoroughly,
bacteria, refrigerated

Healthy Cooking Practices 5 (p.25)
1. b   2. a   3. d   4. c

Diet Myths, Alts. & Choices 1 (p.26)
1. T   2. T   3. T
4. F   5. T

Diet Myths, Alts. & Choices 2–3 (p. 26)
Answers will vary.

Diet Myths, Alts. & Choices 4 (p.26)
A macrobiotic diet is a vegetarian
diet based on brown rice and
whole grains, and it uses only the
vegetables and fruits that are native
to the region in which a person lives.
It is believed that eating native foods
will provide superior nutrition for
living in that particular environment.

Diet Myths, Alts. & Choices 5 (p.26)
1. chicken soup, orange juice
2. liver, kale, spinach
3. dairy products fortified with
   vitamin D

On the Road 1–3 (p. 27)
Answers will vary.

On the Road 4 (p. 27)
2 or 3 are the smarter choices

On the Road 5 (p. 27)
1. 130 c, 5 f   2. 178 c, 13 f
3. 200 c, 9 f   4. 200 c, 0 f
5. 175 c, 4 f   6. 270 c, 6 f
7. 120 c, 8 f   8. 125 c, 0 f
9. 100 c, 10 f   10. 150 c, 1 f
11. 150 c, 5 f   12. 325 c, 15 f

Restaurants 1 (p. 28)
1. 560 c, 30 f   2. 610 c, 29 f
3. 320 c, 16 f   4. 430 c, 12 f
5. 15 c, 0 f   6. 280 c, 17 f
7. 220 c, 4.5 f   8. 360 c, 10 f
9. 270 c, 11 f   10. 590 c, 23 f

Restaurants 2 (p. 28)
1. F   2. F   3. T   4. T

Restaurants 3–4 (p. 28)
Answers will vary.

Restaurants 5 (p. 28)
Healthier choices include spring
mix greens, olives, Italian dressing,
peppers, garbanzo beans, onions,
cherry tomatoes, and cucumbers.

Overeating 1 (p. 29)
All are possible stressors.

Overeating 2–3 (p. 29)
Answers will vary.

Overeating 4 (p. 29)
portion control

Overeating 5 (p. 29)
Answers will vary.

Change Your Behavior 1–4 (p. 30)
Answers will vary.

Change Your Behavior 5 (p. 30)
d. Most experts say you need at least
   21 days to learn a new behavior.
   Individual times may vary.

Dieting Disasters 1 (p. 31)
This is starving. Your body does not
get enough nutrition.

Dieting Disasters 2 (p. 31)
When you eliminate a food group,
you are eliminating the full range of
nutrients.

Dieting Disasters 3 (p. 31)
Supplements are not regulated. There could be disastrous side effects—even death.

Dieting Disasters 4 (p. 31)
Also starvation. Not enough nutrients, and losing weight that fast means it's usually water, not fat.

Dieting Disasters 5 (p. 31)
Nothing can replace exercise to build muscle. Muscle burns more calories faster.

Dieting Wonder Drugs? 1 (p. 32)
A drug has undergone extensive testing for effectiveness and safety and passed the FDA review board. A dietary supplement has had no testing and doesn't have to prove that it does what it claims.

Dieting Wonder Drugs? 2 (p. 32)
The Federal Drug Administration enforces rules to make drugs safe for people to use. A dietary supplement is considered a 'food,' and is not intended to treat or cure a disease.

Dieting Wonder Drugs? 3 (p. 32)
fiber

Dieting Wonder Drugs? 4 (p. 32)
Answers will vary.

Dieting Wonder Drugs? 5 (p. 32)
1. F, 2004   2. T   3. T   4. T

Allergies & Health Issues 1 (p. 33)
Possible reactions include difficulty breathing, swollen lips, difficulty swallowing, itching, hives, sneezing, runny nose, and coughing.

Allergies & Health Issues 2 (p. 33)
1. corn   2. wheat
3. eggs   4. soybeans
5. cow's milk   6. peanuts
7. shellfish

Allergies & Health Issues 3 (p. 33)
Anaphylactic shock is a severe reaction to an allergy marked by difficulty breathing, coughing, swelling of the mouth and throat, hives, tingling, itching, or a metallic taste in the mouth. It can also cause a severe drop in blood pressure and a loss of consciousness.

Allergies & Health Issues 4 (p. 33)
You might have to test your blood sugar regularly, control the amount of sugar and carbohydrates you eat, and inject yourself with insulin.

Allergies & Health Issues 5 (p. 33)
A diet high in saturated and trans fats, as well as cholesterol, can raise the amount of cholesterol in your body. By reducing or eliminating these fats, your cholesterol numbers should drop.

Fitness Facts 1 (p. 34)
1. F   2. T   3. T
4. F, 37% don't   5. T

Fitness Facts 2 (p. 34)
1. 166   2. 60   3. 103
4. 145   5. 54   6. 103

Fitness Facts 3 (p. 34)
c

Fitness Facts 4 (p. 34)
1 and 3 are both correct. Because they are still growing, it is not recommended that children lose more than one pound a month.

Fitness Facts 5 (p. 34)
d

Do You Know? 1 (p. 35)
A calorie is a unit measuring the energy in food.
Calorie count is a measure of the energy derivable from a food source—the total number of calories available.

Do You Know? 2 (p. 35)
You must expend more calories than you take in.

Do You Know? 3 (p. 35)
1. loose   2. layers
3. shoes   4. helmet
5. evaporation

Do You Know? 4 (p. 35)
1. bones and muscles
2. heart and lungs
3. joints

Do You Know? 5 (p. 35)
1. goggles/safety glasses
2. mouth or face guard
3. knee and elbow pads
4. shin guards

Fitness for the Heart 1 (p. 36)
Regular exercise strengthens the heart muscle.

Fitness for the Heart 2 (p. 36)
3, 5, week, 20, 30

Fitness for the Heart 3 (p. 36)
All forms of exercise are good for your heart. Anything that gets the blood pumping is good for the heart!

Fitness for the Heart 4 (p. 36)
Answers will vary.

Fitness for the Heart 5 (p. 36)
1. 45 to 60, five
2. 10 to 12
3. 30 to 35
4. 10 to 12

The Benefits of Exercise 1 (p. 37)
stress, chemicals, brain, dopamine, calming, anxiety

The Benefits of Exercise 2 (p. 37)
chronic, denser, pressure, cholesterol, lowers, protects

The Benefits of Exercise 3 (p. 37)
manage, weight, metabolism, calorie, exercise, diabetes

The Benefits of Exercise 4 (p. 37)
sleep, difficulty, exercise, release, muscles, restful

The Benefits of Exercise 5 (p. 37)
socialize, commitment, climbing, lessons

Journaling 1–5 (p. 38)
Answers will vary.